A More Tender Ocean

A More Tender Ocean

Natalee Caple

Coach House Books

Copyright © Natalee Caple, 2000

first edition

Published with the assistance of the Canada Council for the Arts and the Ontario Arts Council.

CANADIAN CATALOGUING IN PUBLICATION DATA

Caple, Natalee, 1970-
   A More Tender Ocean

Poems.
ISBN 1-55245-057-0

I. Title.

PS8555.A5583M67 2000   C811'54   C00-932864-5
PR9199.3.C36M67 2000

This book is for Christian.

We shall seek a third tiger. This
Will be like those others a shape
Of my dreaming, a system of words
A man makes and not the vertebrate tiger
That, beyond the mythologies,
Is treading the earth.

— Jorge Luis Borges, 'The Other Tiger'

Contents

André Breton You Never Think 11
My Generation Writing of the News on Paper 13
This New Thing Adulthood 14
The Shadow of a Fish 15
The Climate of War 16
'For you and I are helpless' 17
'We took each other in the night' 18
'On the first morning of the world' 19
A More Tender Ocean 20
A Pure Poem 26
Walking Down the Street in Love 27
'A semaphore for seahorses' 28
'A man rents two apartments' 29
'A cupboard and a wooden soldier' 30
The Horse and His Man 31
Your Father's Death 32
'My chief amusement was to lie naked' 33
Poor Girl 34
Polite Aside 35
'Cream as of the night' 36
Twenty Things 37
'The moon is an emerald' 38
The Straw Knight's Fallen Leaves 39
'Be lenient with me' 40
Something Visible 41
In the Tunnels 42
Love Song 44
On the Harmony of the Spheres 45
Begin 46
Begin Again 47
'Love is a bright form of murder' 48
Behind the Kindling Silence 49

It was a Rumour   51
'At his arraignment'   52
Interrogation of a Small White Room   53
People are Brave   54
Two Poems for a Lost Summer   55
'Speak to me more falsely'   56
'How can I explain'   57
'The sky darkening purple'   58
Forgiveness   60
'Why do the hearts of the dead'   61
'Cathedral sky'   62
Filial Knowledge   63
Be Quiet   64
'The separation of curtain after curtain'   65
October When the Sun Sets   66
'I was walking'   67
Comfort   68
Introduction   69
Six Pears   70
Harmonica   71
Good Night   72
'As quick as a camera'   73
'What unrolls?'   74
Normandy   75
Spain   76
L'Oiseau Tzigane   78
Terra Incognita to Say the Way   80
'I am no longer ashamed'   81

André Breton You Never Think

This hand is your brother's   The sun rising out of his palm
    You are jealous
The swinging blades of many things alive in your head
The moon, the assailants
fire in your hands

Who can forget
the story of the criminal making love to a very young girl
in the elevator of her parents' apartment building?
    André Breton

Stripes going all the way down through his shirt to his organs

Cables aching and creaking in the shaft

And she, pressed up against the buttons, half kicking, half crawling
whispering to him:
'You. You.'

What goes on seems ordinary

And when she lay in bed that night, beds and night meaning
something new
She touches her mouth again and again   She feels the unwinding the
unravelling inside of her
Something long sleeping beginning to wake
as it wakes beginning to cry out

She falls on the floor
    She prays
And he wherever, sleeping, *sleeping* as her body howls:

'My love, a wild dog tearing me to shreds. Leaning over me
as I gasp and I am gasping and bleeding away
Not meant to lie quiet and good between the sheets
growing gradually, softly, and smiling
I am shaken   I die in its jaws, holding onto its muzzle
crying: I love you I love you I love you.'

The emptiness, what goes on and on   This is all that there is to knowing someone

The city unfolding to hide him
The criminal calm of his arms, his legs, his back
undirected, absolved, deep into another elevator, waiting in the dark

I wonder if she will ever recover him

My Generation Writing of the News on Paper

We must be quick and delicate   return to the guards
some sense of self-esteem
remember our shadow doves and the flight patterns that
we meant for them

And the dinner is getting cold as the family sleeps
heads buried in unfeathered chests

    Now is the time to write it down

To be proud of being afraid and not afraid —

The youth and destinies of our men have deserted them
Left behind a restaurant breakfast   Round and red and
ill-desired

Say good-bye to your wife
Don't let yourself feel regret

This too is fanciful   This too is the theme of love

Quick and delicate and nothing short of a tremendous
loss of blood could echo in the body or fit the pain in the
voices of these new children

This New Thing Adulthood

Dim with rumours all weeping things made docile by a new beginning.

We'd like to belong. We'd like to be trusted.

But we have no choice the future pops out unexpectedly one minute right after the other. And all the execrations of anger fade with surprise.

We grew tired of waiting. The policeman exited the building.
Our parents finally fell asleep.

And we took on our adult lives grieving every minute for the heroes we'd expected.

The Shadow of a Fish

The shadow of a fish
weighs what does the shadow of a man

Likewise for the fish's dreams
if he has any hopes those too

The man believes in the fish
but the fish does not believe in the man
and the water knows nothing of either of them

The grass holds a mark and a smell of whatever lays
there but cannot be said to know

These are complicated relationships
These are lonely things
and if thinking should be light
the lungs do not hurt for breathing the way that they ache
for thought

The Climate of War

Therefore the property of intelligence will be scattered across these events and although they are heavy may they accumulate some lightness and humour to call back the birdsongs that used to explain them.

And therefore let the skins of lovers who have become foreign to each other touch again and let them melt warmly under the summer sky. There is no need for romance when tender arms and legs open to echo the morning's effect on the climbing orange rose.

And let her mouth swell and let every word be suffocated by his kiss and let his hands seem larger and surer than they were before. And let us forgive the too quick gropings of half-nights half-purchased in the sad burnt days of fall and let the spasming continue for a full minute after the clock has gone quiet.

And let the grass tangle in her hair and stick her eyes and catch beneath her clothes so that she has no good answer for her mother except to run upstairs. And let this be the first afternoon that the boy comes inside her
with radiance
and then let him be quiet. Let him be quiet.

•

For you and I are helpless in the rain fragile as a bare wrist warm as a fresh cut quiet as a new prisoner

                                        tangled in the thorns escaping.

•

We took each other in the night and fell asleep
you still inside me
the snow falling soundlessly upon the roof
the glass of water half drunk upon the night table
beside the silver O of a bracelet

•

On the first morning of the world you lay naked beside a wax
animal

The confusion of substance still to be resolved

The scraps of sky appearing between your eyelashes
as a ragged blue dress
The residue of creation a slick film of sweat over the strange
curves of your breasts
and over the grass in which you lay

Emerald filaments of tragic
       thinness

And this was before the conspirators when you could touch
       yourself
with such impolitic softness under the sun's impassive heat

And the ash of your arousal carried on your skin for hours

A More Tender Ocean

I

It was the first thing, the very first thing that you ever said
It was deep in an impenetrable forest
It was the sound of a hat falling it was the colour of a heart beating
It was surrounded by you

Listen to me

It was painfully light in my mouth

II

How many days on the back of the tortoise?
Crawl along the blazing beach
Think only of the water

His feet made harder each step, and you, tied
up and towed along behind him
leave the greater trail

(What could you desire more than this?)

Everyone you love is initiated
into the conspiracy against you
that you have designed

He is getting tired. The sun is too hot, is
too steady

Listen to me
I love you

III

Freedom is forgetting
The therapist in a chair far too large for him
inciting amnesia
resurrecting exactly the right devil
The patient falling on her knees to welcome the devil home

The night is sad and friendly and your dreams are sad and friendly
It only makes sense
that this aching would mean something in any language
And yet there are more times when your own foreign heart is deaf and mute
What could you rattle loud enough to wake yourself
weak as you are
deep in the night?

IV

Your voice is prehensile

Through the beer glasses and the smoke
the cracked backs of wooden chairs
the coughing and the whispering

I feel the sharp dive   the erotic unwinding
Sweet white meat of Japanese poison fish
And it is my heavy eyelids that your voice pries open
my soft fears
my lips swollen
and unsure
Don't leave   Don't leave
I'll go and get a bottle of rubies
I'll bring back handfuls of wine
I can make you happy
Trust me   it tastes like metal
but it isn't

V

Invertebrate lovers in a clay pot
interrupted by a sudden rain
Their bodies roll
impatiently
Nothing political about sex buried in the wet
brown earth

VI

There was a man
deep in an impenetrable forest
alone with his hat and an apple
And his wife stole his hat
(his favourite hat)
and the apple rolled away – what can you do?
Weep until the sky turns to glass and the wind shatters the glass
until the glass sky rains down to silence you
He lay down and the earth was disgruntled beneath him but
the leaves gathered over him
with the sublime neutrality of anything real
The man became a leafy bump
something you would never offer anything to
And he was happier even if you don't believe me

A Pure Poem

And the last door lay open to the lightest touch of fingers
All the long wooden pews of a church piled high
with fresh exotic fruit   A politician asleep stretched out with
his head in the red silk lap of a bishop and the choir singing softly
not to wake him but to help him dream

A thousand winds like paraffin and long blue fields of wool

Walking Down the Street in Love

Walking down the street in love the gentleman said, 'That's where it began'. And there was some reality to his accusation. His footsteps echoed the same sentiments as his words. And then the gentleman said, 'I do not know what you are talking about. But rest assured, I will not tell a soul, not even if I am tortured. We must be most loyal to the ones we do not know'. And I was pleased but felt that night with the streetlamps just then coming on that I could not trust him and so I smiled and said to him, 'Sir, you must be so in love'.

•

A semaphore for seahorses a necklace of electric eels. A series of tiny white signals across the ocean of tiny peaks. A yellow shadow in the centre of an orchid. The dreams of a happy man in prison. The man walks up to the door of a building and the building crumbles away. The man's wife is waiting for him in their bed, his infant daughter asleep beside her. Now they are both asleep. His wife's hand is open. The lines of her hand are a map that he could remember if he could hold on for one second longer.

•

A man rents two apartments. One right above the other on the corner of a brick building. On the first day that he moves into the downstairs apartment he drills a hole through the ceiling, through the floor, of his two homes. The telephone rings, he murmurs instructions. He has bought a large piece of cork and he sits on the floor in the afternoon whittling the cork to fit the hole. The landlord lets someone into the building to see him.

Why do you have two apartments, his friend asks.

He smiles and walks over to the cork in the ceiling. He pulls the cork out and after a rumble of adjustment an orange falls down through the hole into his outstretched hand. He catches two oranges and quickly plugs the hole again. He offers one orange to his friend.

•

A cupboard and a wooden soldier in the cupboard and in the tummy of the soldier a long pink rolling worm. The magnified scales of the worm look like the folds of a satin dress slick with sweat from dancing all night. The tiny drop of sweat shivers as if on the tip of a young woman's breast and her breast reminds you of her knees and her knees remind you of the sensation in your hands the first time that you touched her. The first time that you touched her like the first time that you became aware of yourself in the world as an infant touching your mother's breast in the middle of the night after drawing her to you by crying out with sudden lonesomeness.

The Horse and His Man

A horse washed out to the ocean
and his man was left alone on the beach
weeping for the horse

'More than water, more than a red tree
more than language, or a handful of glass birds,'

(he called)

'I want you between my knees moving
like the first brilliant thought.'

Your Father's Death

What I remember about the apple trees is the hardness of the apples
and how they fell over me when you were climbing

Your father's unease so swiftly met by my candid glance
I knew that he only wanted to hold me and to have me open my blouse

Who would have thought that a man like that
or any man   could drown in the rain standing out in a field calling
for his teenage son in the middle of a storm

There are worse things that I could do to you than your father imagined
Sickly old dog   Miserly lover   Evil empty-headed man

Why do you grieve for him?

•

My chief amusement was to lie naked in a field and wait for you.

I am hungry! I am heavy with my house of innocent stones!

I stained you with my tongue for you grew tired of me and you dove down and punished me for the wet day does not own the bear and the jet sky does not own the hours and I was drunk with all the constellations of your thoughts.

You built a monument of gold to honour me and then you bit at it with your teeth until it was ridiculous.

And you made me sinister and unholy and you took me once more before you left.

Poor Girl

If you had a woman in the grave with you would your hands be rough?

And if you spilt beer on the blouse of a woman who was afraid of birds and alone in a bar how would your words reassure her?

And if she started to cry and said that she was dying would you lay her down upon the floor and kiss her hair?

Her long black hair so soon to disappear and her white stomach with her wet blouse pulled out from the band of her skirt.

And if she said, 'I'm dying. Make love to me in front of your friends'. How would you begin?

Polite Aside

Clean your teeth with a twig
you meaningless mutt
I see a portico and fifteen guards
waiting for you

Like a king on your throne
you grin at me
Aroma of swine
putrefaction of form
your manhood a fig
no more memorable than
the finger of a beggar

∙

Cream as of the night   he fell over daylight
and the lamp became forgotten   Spent pillows clutched into loss
A hazardous delay   The moon rose
a catalogue of hours   starspent perfecting the motion

a limp memory of poverty   bare skin in the afternoons of wood

and the bold arms which   misthrew you
re-enter your dreams   bleached mastery

An orchidal lament   for mouths full of water
sea-claw vagina   not counting
and twisting warm oysters   The bed does not grieve

                    the cleaved air

Twenty Things

An invisible passage
image of a door

The pulse at the elbow
grey wisps of cobwebs

almond sunset
in the west
sand in toes of shoes
soft washing of waves on the shore
green glass bottle

icicles dripping into the snow
clean pressed sheets

a crinkling map
newspaper
coffee grounds
a warm bath
in the quiet house

fire in the stone fireplace
fingers made bare

lemon cake
stomach ache

eyelashes falling
a smile opening

into a promise
dark as your only horse

•

The moon is an emerald turned pale with desire and its hypnotic light shines upon the wiry gold of a bird's nest turned around in a treetop over the blue mountain peaks the bodies of two virgin children wrapped around each other discovering in the cold winter night a tender and confusing source of heat.

The moon is the palm of a woman's hand noble and slender as she strokes herself in the deep deaf sheets of a stranger's bed.

The moon is a word that you opened your mouth to speak to me just as my eyelids trembled shut.

The open wound of an eye of the dark bruise of the moon appearing in a dream as a whisper in the ear of the queen of wasps. O her stinger shudders with honeyed love for the sapphire of her husband's tongue.

The moon is a tear caught by a tongue.

The Straw Knight's Fallen Leaves

At night we play affectionate games
like birds pushing apples along the stone road with their beaks
The steam rises out of the kitchen to cloud the memory of your
favourite painter

Contagious tears flow between us

And your bare legs in your swim trunks cast a long shadow
and the water is smooth as silk pyjamas

The dangerous air peeks under my clothes at the sleeves
The eyebrows of sculptures
     raising
Laughter furry with love
Tremendous icebergs of lace

•

Be lenient with me

(Tiny white signals
too small to be photographed)

I make no music
(Exposed by the wind)

I do not claim to suffer

To spur the sorrow
(Blue one I never meant to love)

The birds I have kept hidden in my attic
are quiet now

Something Visible

For three years the pale knees of heaven

and the cave brilliant with amandines

his hand under her breast   her arm twisted under her

'Where is my dog?'

the porpoise fed upon the panther

the pink shine of her engorged clitoris

but a man must pay his taxes

and all the small finches asleep on the branches

he lay by the cliff edge

he stared at the lemon boats

and she ate all the pomegranate seeds

Such larceny

to call a girl a genius a girl

'Who is that splashing?'

The pattern of her dress made supple with the breeze

'Come and kiss me. Kiss my dirty mouth.'

In the Tunnels

There was a couple in the time when trains had sleeper cars. The coupling of strangers was common in the overcrowded cars. Twice a month, travelling away from the evening lamps of one European city toward the morning lamps of another, they would meet and flail under the grey wool of passing time.

They did not really know each other and so in his mind he called her[1] sometimes Sylvia and sometimes Jane. In their presence the bodies remembered each other but later his mind could only recall certain parts of her clearly: her crooked teeth, her soft[2] black hair, her stomach swollen and glowing under the tiny reading light (the landscape rocking away outside the window, as the cots rocked along in the car).

And the years passed and they met and flailed and eventually something unseen began to take a different shape. Their lovemaking became more referential; as if in the tossing and clawing you could make out the voice[3] of your best friend saying[4], 'Do you remember when … '

'Yes[5]. And do you remember … '

And if you couldn't call this love[6], then there was still something to it, a kind of sharp bright[7] tenderness that would make the man's throat tighten whenever he thought about it while he was alone.

One day something happened to the woman. He never found out what. He had some premonition of it as he ran to catch the train, his taxi slow, his wife crying[8] as he left; and he, holding her face[9], recalling the vestigial guilt that all good businessmen cultivate. He was running and sweating and suddenly, before he even saw the foreign faces conversing mildly in their lost car, he felt then the sense of an ending.

What is it about love that it does not realize itself when it should but only when it can? Love running all through the night calling[10] and calling to its object, 'Return to me. Return to me, I know you now.[11]'

1 her
2 soft
3 voice
4 saying
5 yes
6 this love
7 sharp bright
8 his wife crying
9 holding her face
10 running all through the night, calling
11 Return to me. Return to me. I know you now.

Love Song

A delinquent display
spread of the branches like a hand held up against the sun   A magnet and a mirror

A blackbird tucked between the breasts of a large dark woman

The instantaneous incarnations of sex in the diaphanous afternoon
    shadows

You must be breathing now, even as I think of you my quick fish

my black lung
my soft crevice
my lubricated column
my empty fireplace
my bucket of dirty water
my silly dog
my closing light
my unreadable font
my little love bite
my testicles

On the Harmony of the Spheres

There are two men of equal personal value and for no clear reason you are given a greater perspective on one than on the other.

This one man loves his friend but he feels deprived because he is not aware of his friend's reciprocal feeling. Over the course of a story this man loses his friend again and again. He loses him first when his friend goes mad, and again when his friend commits suicide, and he loses him a third time when he discovers that his friend had betrayed him with his wife.

The friendship of the two men is a heavy glass sphere held in the hands of the surviving man. The glass sphere shatters at the impact of knowledge and the knowledge itself becomes the thousands of silvery shards embedded in the skin of the man's palms and wrists.

It is then that the man realizes that as a discrete object, however greatly valued, the sphere had been at once easier to hold and to put away, and as a shattered object the sphere, which cannot properly be called a sphere anymore, can neither be held nor completely released.

And the distance between one man, his friendship, and his friend closes suddenly in a storm of tiny wounds.

Begin

The house echoes
a confusion of sound or clarity
The still rug and two bodies
half-lit   remote

It is plain the way that the hours sharpen
and the blade of you unreachable
Blood divides us, the rivers
and pulsebeats
The world ripening unreal

Entwined in the absence of syllables
the punctuation of every breath underscored
by a quiet lift of the ribs

This gulf is the opposite of death
and time is a creature with fifteen heads
and no heartbeat

Begin Again

Will the man find his love dead or asleep?
Will the sky be dark or light
murky with fog?

Will the shadows arrange themselves
convenient to interpretation
a tall bird strangling a mirror?

No bullets can wound a shadow

They are the undrawn portraits of the present

A narrow line and evil does not fail to sing
The Germans never really existed   Folklore undoes itself
is its own suicidal memory
The aluminum shiver of
so many
recombinant
childhood fears

•

Love is a bright form of murder   It is what we cannot see
endured like any intoxicant

A brutal wave of thought

Rest rest we shall redress the beautiful movements we
shall learn to touch everything again

with fiery radiance and rockets of quick noise

hands like wind over the long grass plains
all the tigers let loose at once
We cannot hear   We cannot smell

And the adornment of the sun
possessed a harpish glow a deep intake
And each new evening brass and diamonds
soften the purchase of wide green eyes

Behind the Kindling Silence

Behind the kindling silence a girl's tears

the magistrate stern in his robes

footsteps retire down the stone hall

the wet heel of her hand against her cheek

the grey air the abyss

mating rituals of extinct animals

the hump and the spasm

a deeper silence

A shadow moves quietly out of the corner

the girl's legs as if they were broken

her open hands

'I could have told you how to make a man fall in love.'

Her shadowed eyes uncomprehending

It's awful

the landscape outside green and bright the trains still

black to walk so far

to tell you

behind her lips the rags of childhood

a lost face

a bridge of cries

the morning

she took off her dress and forgot herself

It was a Rumour

It was a rumour
that the great dark man they all suspected
had been after her

A little red blossom on a thorny tree
His hands were bleeding
and she stared at him

A crescendo of thunder
collapse of the sky beneath the rain

And they hid together
in an empty barn

Her brothers scoured the landscape
a train of dogs in the farmland harbour
Cornfields washed away

Her mother listened for her
knowing her little heart as if it beat in the air

And she turned on her side
away from the long heat of his body
and began to cry
Infancy resurrected
just before it disappears

He held her shoulder quietly
and listened to the rain
The end of the world   a long time in coming
The morning an unfathomable distance away

•

At his arraignment
the girl whispered into the microphone
some uncertain murmur of love
A niche of flesh
and in the waking light
the position of her deepest want
given away in the newspapers

The easy intervention of one history within another

Because when he recited his crimes
his only defence a puny parachute:
'I could have waited to marry her,' he said
'I could have drunk more wine.'

Interrogation of a Small White Room

Don't approach me
the clandestine sun

and what the soldiers wanted was their father's return

permission
to interrogate the sky

a churning under youthful skins
Clarity of your pupils
the well

afflicted eyes avert
Don't look at me

I am a fever

and for the last afternoon I open my mouth
and you place a skinned plum on my tongue

I caress your fingers
your strange front

words in the water words like subtle fish
swallow the movement of the wave against the sand

diminutive

your heart comes to know defencelessness
lead forward out of the frost
a hand in your hand
in your hand a wet small hand

People are Brave

People are brave
I give up my heart

I say to you that
people are brave

wherever there is blood
and shadow
unique dreams rise out
of the quiet heads of infants

and the thrust of love
like a light through your heart
like a face buried against your neck
and a weight between your thighs

a vision of nightshade

a naked candle reflected in your pupils

People are brave

Two Poems for a Lost Summer

This is my hand

> *You whisper our secret history*

And these are my legs

> *There is no allusion here*

I have counted all the days since I left you

> *As if a clock could be as articulate as the sun*

The changes in the weather so suddenly emancipated into meaning

> *The sky watching over you in my absence*

Metaphors previously unmentioned surfacing undecayed

> *The whole world knows my mistake*

Suddenly aware of the cold

> *And the lakebed holds an imprint of our long-departed summer skins*

We are suddenly aware of the cold

•

Speak to me more falsely
Batter away the insignificant stuttering of your first thought
O what vows I heard you make to the sea
and you bent your head to the red starfish

I have seen
          and so have you
orchids put to shame by sunrise

•

How can I explain to them
the bare bright light of my body surrounding the ghost of your fingers and the sky collapsing in azure fog over the ocean the unbearable ringing of an alarm clock in the depths of your sleep the thinnest dress in creation catching fire where it is draped over your silent antique lamp. At some point I couldn't hear you any more and your assurances were swallowed dull and thick uselessly slow in the static. The water lapping up against the indifferent skin of the shore.
And you ignore me.

•

The sky darkening purple behind a hurricane of opals. My fingers forgotten and then remembered in my mouth.

The water on the windows sliding down, you were behind me. Every occurrence avoided is realized even by my thinking of it. The spindly bodies of ants tumbling down through liquid honey, the bright blue of a crystal held up to the sunlight. Your hands combing through the softness of my hair.

I believe that my skin has the design of rain and the desire of milk flows beneath it. My skin shivering throughout the night.

I believe that your skin has the design of fire and the desire of wine flows beneath it. Your skin turns feverish and glows red in the night.

And the tiny tongues of animals come more readily to you, the sweet rough licking of a kitten at your breast. Such an articulate tremble their reward. The flat bottoms of your feet with maps tattooed upon them and the veins of your legs leading upward to a frictionless gasp, your chest a desert beneath my hand, your mouth a well. Soft buffeting of air as if I had released a dove.

The noise of a glass breaking on the floor of another room.

And when I pinned your arms against the ground you only stared at me. I fell into the damp blank moment and your body, your arousal, was the template for the pensive contractions of my empty heart. Outside the rain battered and enraged upon the earth, the thunder deep and feminine rumbling hungry through the sky. The giant hearts of horses beating hard inside their chests as they ran down the shining street.

What could I give you now? What could I offer you to lie beneath me again and not to fight against me? If I were invisible and only a ghost to avoid your repentance could I touch you again with my hands harmless and slender as leaves?

Like a penny dropped from the bow of a ship over the darkest miles of the ocean tumbling slowly down, revolving through the silence in the absence of light, I am abandoned here.

Forgiveness

Where everything is petrified in its descent and your black mouth sinks swollen full of tears

        The faces of strangers appear in the openings of stone grottos serene even in the sunless tomb

And down you fell through the shaft   through the fissure slow ragged perspective of your surroundings   The glittering naked schist below
and you squint as you stare at the floor
rushing up to greet you

Are you hovering are you exhausted? Was the last burden the last extremity the last fortress built to stream out the vision of your eyes
        There is some small cover over there

Lodged in the corner of your heart the rampant growth of full freedom if you can only metamorphose into something more pensive

coeval of night   venomous ant   tender variation

Complete and vigilant under the sooty embankment straining for the thrum of stars

•

Why do the hearts of the dead beat in the minds of the grieving and the colour grey the grain of the coffin wood the warm wind steeped in symbolism

as the sun seems to signal a more specific message to the man on a raft who can die of thirst in the middle of the ocean?

And why do all the shoes and cloaks and things of the dead not evaporate with their presence but must be touched and remembered and folded away every shirt a wedding gown and every rumpled sheet evidence of a terrible crime.

And why do our names stay the same when our lives are changed the colour of our eyes not deepen with each loss?

And why is the bus schedule not affected? Nor the lust of adolescence nor the weight of commerce nor the measure of the minutes there is no new sound to the universe and the lights don't dim the chairs are all as sturdy as they were before and the length and width of beds and bureaus
    dear friends startled by their own unexpected indifference. The world still spins if it seems to rock.

As if death were a thing of paper and everything accomplished by a life is the reduction of that life to so few lines of print uncorrected on a page and a deep and everlasting sense of shock.

●

Cathedral sky dark as an Australian sapphire
You are beautiful   You are dear

All the little house roofs steaming grey smoke
The shining streets unmarried   The garages tightly closed

A shroud of snow descending over the trees below unaware

The dream of an abandoned bicycle lies slender on the grass
The rotation of the earth speeds forward; we are beginning anew

Letting go of each other as if we were strangers
and stepping out into a foreign night

Filial Knowledge

As if in coming to understand something you believe that thing to be infected with your knowledge of it and its usefulness to you begins to appear structural so that inevitably you begin to assume that the thing you understand must have been created by you and is therefore your property.

The night sky to astronomers and your body to every doctor on the planet.

Purchase through comprehension and the destruction of meaning by desire.

And the deflection of guilt nothing more then an endless conversation between two mirrors in a sunlit room.

Be Quiet

A dry pair of eyes and the wind
    The bed seems so distant now
Eyes are only eyes

And all the doings and undoings of the human heart
dusty with history

The streets begin to taste like fruit

Begin to guess the colour of your children's wishes
Begin to stalk tomorrow's open arms
Your stomach is a beacon; your hunger is the rotating light
And the world is a circle of windows
shuttered by your eyelashes

quiet and deep with the cold

•

The separation of curtain after curtain after curtain of soft mountain fog
        silver as the rain trapped in a bridal veil
                silver as an infant's first winter breath
                      silver as the way I long for sleep the way I long for you asleep
                      beside me

What the garden grass remembers is the rolling shape of children arguing or small summer dogs playing or how many kinds of lovers clawing away at the things that the world begs them to return

The division down the middle of each blade of grass and the way that the wind pauses   The absence of impact
How I miss you   Is how I miss you

October When the Sun Sets

Be an angel fluttering near the lamp at six o'clock
powdery wings so hazardously delicate

And touch my neck beneath my hair
I do need you

The summer is something so round
and yet it runs through your cupped hands
clean and calm and distant from your human thirst

The night comes on with the slowness of a year
Your eyes retreat from mine
tilting like the stars

                      inexhaustible   cheated

and I try to hold on to every good thought

The shapes of trees against the evening sky
The sudden flight of seagulls
Your constant power still unbroken
and every white step shivers
with the glimpse of your feet behind mine

•

I was walking and you were not there the street shining
with black feathers
How could this have happened?
I was sleeping and you were there
I turned to you and asked you:
How could this have happened?
It was the perfect day   You were as soft and mute as summer
I was irradiated by you

The sun was shining all around my bony feet and then a tree fell

The lumberjack said: You better get out of here an omelette is burning
or else a house
and I fled

I never felt any guilt for leaving you behind.
I never felt any guilt for leaving you behind.
I never felt any guilt for leaving you behind.
I never felt any guilt for leaving you behind.
I never felt any guilt for leaving you behind.

Comfort

Aubergine the word you used
I didn't understand what caused your dreams
The sound of the tide rising overwhelmed your voice
What were trying to tell me?

O come a little way in
closer to the shore

I will cover you up with a silver bell
lined with unsparing velvet
I will listen all night with my ear to the bell
to catch every word of your fears

Introduction

We	like the birds are charmed from the treetops by the postman
We	emerge from wan bedchambers to yawn at the darkness
We	tear away from the grasp of true love
We	ride wooden horses
We	sigh to glimpse red and white petals mingle in our children's palms
We	lie down in front of locomotives
We	love hyacinths
We	signal each other
We	extend our wings and cry out when the buildings collapse
We	metamorphose (staircase) into (starlight)
We	stare down the gap behind the bed
We	tickle and bite
We	lie motionless together
We	wrap towels around our hair
We	have seven main configurations for pleasure
We	give words to vagabonds
We	are so happy to meet you

Six Pears

Six pears like sleeping children
by the riverbank

Dance like a swallow in the night

And in your yellow dress
so beautiful and vain

your frigid breasts held high to show the moon
Happiness is simply the trembling skin
the frozen moment of her forehead

The wet vowel in the middle of a
word suddenly hushed

A small sound instantly forgotten

Harmonica

Monica sweet tourmaline
you are already brilliant
at the bottom of the pond

You are already quick
between the trees

To look at you the
weakness of a tiger
The feeling of a being
being undone

Good Night

Good night
it will be hours until
you open your eyes again

Good night
the stars are waiting for
your light to dim

It will be a long night
when you leave

It will be a long night
when the earth forgets you

Every flower furls
beneath the heat of your dreams

Tomorrow will be bright
sweet day

Good night

•

As quick as a camera shutter opening and closing a small cat appears and then disappears again by your feet. You look up at the ceiling and see the bright fog of stars that you remember from the countryside. Your back arches for the long wet fingers of grass. You turn your head and someone smiles at you.

'Would you like a piece of cake?' your lover asks and you are kissed by a mouth as soft and warm as lamplight.

•

What unrolls?

The rose

The rolls of haystacks

The field of snow

The hearts of old folks

The word unrolls

Normandy

Leer at the pardoners
the car serves an avian frond

Et lea sang no nougat as
less fueled as a

Noose avows north muscles barbarous
Silence   noise
leavens repaid

erotic   the semblance
of a moose

it is you I forgave

Spain

A seagull the easternly sea
a poorer bath
at last

the cause for collages

a duel, a decimator
a la allegro

pies or pesos venetian a ventaja

hasty as a queen
coo
sit
see
glower

The sale of a Volvo

contra
eel suede

a voice

entices heroic Abuja

and a cafe elf

did see the air

lost among the fruit
a cerise
pear

L'Oiseau Tzigane
The Gypsy Bird

Je découvre une étoile blanche dans le ciel violâtre.
I have found one white star in the purplish sky.

Je découvre deux colombes grises dans la marguerite exfoliée.
I have found two grey doves in the naked daisy tree.

Je découvre trois serpents argentés tremblant dans l'hiver.
I have found three silver snakes shivering in the winter.

Je découvre quatre coeurs si doux.
I have found four hearts so tender.

Je découvre cinq roses mortes.
I have found five dead roses.

Je découvre six enfants jouant dans les colchiques.
I have found six children playing in the meadow saffron.

Je découvre sept anges couchant près de mon amour.
I have found seven angels sleeping by my love.

Je découvre huit faons frolés par les ombres.
I have found eight fawns brushed by shadows.

Je découvre neuf emeraudes brisées encore une fois.
I have found nine emeralds broken again.

Je découvre dix nuits disparues.
I have found ten nights which have disappeared.

Je découvre onze insectes nocturnes sur les belles bouches d'amoureux.
I have found eleven night insects on the pretty mouths of lovers.

Je découvre douze oiseaux bleus qui ne voient pas les femmes nues.
I have found twelve blue birds who do not see the naked women.

Je découvre treize ciels sans soleil.
I have found thirteen sunless skies.

Je découvre quatorze colombes épousées éternellement.
I have found fourteen doves forever married.

Je découvre quinze feuilles chères après la lumière claire d'aurore.
I have found fifteen dear leaves after the pure light of daybreak.

•

Voici le gage de mon amour, ces lumières bestiales, souvenir des glaciers génies.

Terra Incognita to Say the Way

Don't make me say it	to break	your charm
wandering hands of light	the quick	breath penetrate
A waking dream	that torn dress	my dress
Kiss me	Kiss me again	again
you know	I adore you	The night
the dark trees	the silver lake	swallowing
the flow	of one	thought breaking

•

I am no longer ashamed of my hands
    around me the warm waves boundless green hearts
    under the star-fogged sky

I am no longer ashamed of my mouth
    wherever I go angels fall in love with me

Light fingers of angels gold green tips of tiny tongues

I am no longer ashamed of my shoulders
    transparent wordless the wind cries out like butter
    the knees I hid beneath my hand I reveal to you now
    empty cavern aching for the sun the sheer black shale of
    memory

Stand before the broken light
    my cloudy hair cheeks afire
    open door where the ocean comes in

Undertow of a hollow dream

And I will sit beside you on the bed
    don't be afraid

    agate blue
    the lace of stuttered breaths

Dedications

'My Generation Writing of the News on Paper' and 'The Climate of War' are for Kenneth Patchen.
'On the Harmony of the Spheres' is for Salman Rushdie.
'Harmonica' is for Monica Panhuyzen.
'Introduction' is for Zane Mo Iseman on the occasion of his birth.
'Good Night' is for Mali and Lesje Caple.
'L'Oiseau Tzigane' is for Christian Bök and Guillaume Apollinaire.
'Twenty Things' is for George Samuel Caple.

Acknowledgements

The author gratefully acknowledges the assistance of the Ontario Arts Council and the Toronto Arts Council for providing financial assistance towards the completion of this book.

For his generous support and for the final proof of this book I thank my friend and editor Darren Wershler-Henry. For their effort and skill in bringing this book to print I Would thank Stan Bevington, damian lopes, Rick/Simon and Alana Wilcox. For accompanying me day and night I thank my consort Christian Bök. For their love and support I thank my family: Mali, Lesje, Patricia, Russell and Suzanne Caple, Philippa and Gwyneth Probyn, Eileen Caple, Joyce Thomas, Marc Hicks and Nick Kazamia. For their advice and assistance with this manuscript in various stages I thank Kelly Ryan, Martha Sharpe, Erin Mouré, Michael Holmes, Christopher Dewdney, David and Edna Magder, Stephen Cain, Suzanne and Phil Zelazo. For the use of the astonishing photograph on the cover of this book I thank Michael Ondaatje.

Poems that appear in this book have appeared previously in: above/ground press broadsides and chapbooks, *Canadian Literature*, *The Lazy Writer*, *The Little York Review (lit)*, *Matrix*, *paperplates*, *Plus Zero*, *Queen Street Quarterly*, *Rampike*, *Sub-Terrain*, *Torque* and *West Coast Line*.

Typeset in Spectrum
Printed at the Coach House Press on bpNichol Lane

Edited by Darren Wershler-Henry
Designed by damian lopes
Cover design by Rick/Simon
Cover photo by Michael Ondaatje

To read the online version of this text and other titles from Coach House Books, visit our website:
www.chbooks.com

To add your name to our e-mailing list, write:
mail@chbooks.com

Toll free:
1 800 376 6360

Coach House Books
401 Huron Street (rear) on bpNichol Lane
Toronto, Ontario
M5S 2G5

Reading Natalee Caple's poetry, you find yourself in a dreamscape – both familiar and strange. A man rents an apartment and fills it with oranges. Two strangers make love on a train. All the names for water are here, beside electric eels, philosophical fish, tigers let loose in rain. This is an astonishing first book of poems, unsettling in its intimacy; the poetry flickers and pulses in the unconscious, insisting on sea change, a more tender ocean.
    – Esta Spalding

'What goes on seems ordinary' in Natalee Caple's poems but isn't, like taking vitamins in the dark and finding out they are amphetamines, or alphabetamines, small enumerations of pleasure loss risk speech sexualities touches wonders transfigurations streets meadows rains, 'the city unfolding' and 'her body howls'. No wonder, for here fairy-tale tonalities coincide with real life and waking … it's wonderful, tremulous, etched with absolute acute simplicity.
    – Erin Mouré

These poems fill me with joy – their light touch, their deft weaving thru the traffic of human relations & misconnections, their open gaze, their heart. Natalee Caple is a gifted writer; someone to watch.
    – Di Brandt